The BASEBALL FIELD
at NIGHT

The BASEBALL FIELD
at NIGHT

last poems

PATRICIA GOEDICKE

LOST HORSE PRESS

SANDPOINT · IDAHO

Edited by Christopher Howell.
Cover art by William Robert Johnston.
Author photo courtesy of University of Montana, University Relations Department.
Cover and interior design by Christine Holbert.

This and other fine Lost Horse Press titles may be viewed online at www.losthorsepress.org.

FIRST EDITION

Library of Congress Cataloging-in-Publication Data

Goedicke, Patricia.
 The baseball field at night : last poems / by Patricia Goedicke.—1st ed.
    p. cm.
ISBN 978-0-9762114-8-8 (alk. paper)
I. Title.
PS3557.O32B37 2008
811'.54—dc22
            2007044333.

ACKNOWLEDGMENTS

With love and thanks always to my fine, insightful readers, poets Sarah Gridley and Melissa Kwasny, to my dear, long-time friends Connie Poten and Dee McNamer, and with thanks also to the editors of the following magazines for publishing, some of them in slightly different form, the following poems:

ACM/Another Chicago Magazine: "The Treasure," "Sooner Speak to the Moon"

AGNI: "From the Book of Small Animals"

Alligator Juniper: "Night Notes" and "Moon Song"

Beloit Poetry Journal: "Hole"

The Denver Quarterly: "The Baseball Field at Night"

Elevated Living: "Cloud Chamber and Circumference"

Evensong: Contemporary Poems of Spirituality: "Aftermath," "Except at the Window" and "Unicycles of the Dead"

Eventsky: "The Baseball Field at Night"

The Gettysburg Review: "The City of In Between," "Heliopause in His Study Now Her Bedroom" and "The Blow"

The Green Mountains Review: "Aftermath: Pinpoint and Torrent"

The Hampden Sydney Review: "Each Moment"

Hayden's Ferry Review: "Letter to . . ."

Hubbub: "In the Neighborhood"

The Hudson Review: "Vegetable 69"

The Manhattan Review: "Cloud Chamber and Circumference"

The North Dakota Review: "L'Chaim"

Poetry Southeast: "This Music Has Holes in It"

Poetry Daily: "The Blow"

Prairie Schooner: "Unicycles of the Dead"

Redactions: "Trace"

The Seneca Review: "Kalo Taxidi, Fuera Y Maintenant"

Southeast Poetry Review: "This Music Has Holes in It"

Square Lake: "This Music Has Holes in It"

Volt: "The Body," "Trompe l'Oeil," "Death Song, Dolce, Dolce" and "Except at the Window"

In Memoriam by Melissa Kwasny was first published in *Drumlummon Views* and *NEO.*

TABLE *of* CONTENTS

for Leonard Wallace Robinson
still here

On July 4, 2006, poet Patricia Goedicke died of complications from cancer at the age of seventy-five. The day before, her hospital bed in Missoula was strewn with a copy of Dante's *Inferno*, the latest *New York Times Book Review*, and several printouts from *Drumlummon Views*. Novelists, poets, friends, and former students came in and out, singing, reading, discussing the news of the Israeli invasion of Lebanon, an event she was particularly concerned with because her sister, Jeane-Marie Cook, was living in Beirut. She was, as we say, *in medias res*, in the middle of the action, action which was always emotionally engaged, passionately intellectual, and literary.

Patricia's many friends will miss how she would answer her door, high heels clacking in excitement, all dressed up, red lipstick on. She loved company! She knew how to take delight: in the yellow summer dress in a shop window on Higgins, sauvignon blanc and her backyard swing at dusk, music—she was a member of two choirs her last winter—and talk of poetry, more delightful than anything, what she could do for hours. (Patricia told a friend that ink fresh off the printer smelled like forsythia.) She kept a round table in her living room piled with hundreds of books of poetry she had recently acquired, a treasure trove that often functioned as a lending library. For years, her graduate workshops met in her home with its books and art, flowers and piano, the photograph of a young, black-haired Patricia talking to Robert Frost.

She was born Patricia Ann McKenna in Boston on June 2, 1931, and grew up in Hanover, New Hampshire, where her father was a neurologist and a professor at Dartmouth. She was educated at Middlebury College and Ohio University. In 1957, she married Victor Goedicke, whom she divorced twelve years later. In between, she met her lifelong friend Pat Grean and began to publish. *Between Oceans*, her first book of poems, appeared in 1968, the year she married Leonard Wallace Robinson, *Esquire* fiction editor and writer for the *New Yorker*, whom she met playing ping-pong at the MacDowell Colony. The couple moved to San Miguel de Allende, Mexico during the 1970s and returned in 1982 when Patricia took a teaching position at The University of Montana, where she taught until her death. She was the recipient of a National Endowment of the Arts fellowship, a Rockefeller Foundation Residency in Bellagio, Italy, the William Carlos Williams Prize, and the H. G. Merriam Award for contributions to literature in Montana, among many honors.

How does one speak of the work—because it is the work, in addition to her great love for Leonard and her tireless, generous, inspired teaching, that was central to Patricia's life—in a career that spans thirty-eight years, or one that is this prolific—twelve books, including *Crossing the Same River, The Wind of Our Going, The Tongues We Speak* (a *New York Times* Notable Book in 1990), *Invisible Horses*, and *When Earth Begins to End* (selected by the American Library Association as one of the top ten books of poetry in 2000). Revising furiously through the once-a-week chemotherapy treatments, she finished her thirteenth manuscript, *The Baseball Field at Night*, weeks before entering the hospital. In addition, there seemed to be no subject Patricia was uninterested in—cats, classical music, politics, string theory, skiing (she was a downhill racer) or anything she would flinch from—illness, aging, grief, death, marital arguments. Many of the books are over a hundred pages long and many poems five or six pages. Still, there are certain currents in her writing one can trace across the many books: her deep love for her second husband Leonard, "the one man / I always meant to love and now can," the body's indignities and triumphs, death. Love and loss—the two great themes of poetry—are ones she tackled with originality, grit, unflinching courage, and amplitude.

The day after Deirdre McNamer gave me word of Patricia's death, I asked to read a poem of hers, "What Rushes Past Us," at dinner at the writer's colony on Whidbey Island where I was staying:

> Every newspaper headline, every last quarrel
> We ever had, each hangover, each miraculous glass
> of the deep bourbon of love, even the pure silence of prayer
> Is pouring past us like rain

The writers at the table with me were surprised, because it seemed so prescient, to hear she had written it in 1985.

> The wind roars in our ears, in the dizzy whirl of the blood
> There's no turning back, on parallel tracks shooting
> From the cliff of our birth we keep falling
> First you, then me, then me rushing by you.

But Patricia wrote about death always, its imminence and immanence. It is a dominant theme through all her work, not surprisingly so, given her life. Her mother died of breast cancer when Patricia was thirty-nine. Her father suffered from lung cancer and multiple sclerosis. Patricia was first diagnosed with breast cancer when she was living in Mexico. She would battle cancer all her life, surviving two mastectomies, and finally succumbing to cancer which had spread to her lungs, spine, and liver. Leonard was twenty years her senior and would die before her, in 1999. Death was indeed "her home light," as she writes in "Trompe L'Oeil."

The poetry, paradoxically, is not morbid nor falsely transcendent. It is fiercely honest, clear-headed, tough-minded, audacious. It is also incredibly moving. Patricia might spit at death, as she did many other tragedies of the body—cancer, hot flashes, aging, chemo, bad sex—but she also acknowledged them as deeply human and shared. She protested, stamped her diminutive foot, cried out, and she fought against the odds, as she advises us to do in "For All the Sad Rain":

> There are dogs who keep their skinny tails
> Permanently between their legs
> But also there are sleek horses, as easily as there are curs
> There are squash blossoms that flower around fountains
> Like white butterflies, there is courage everywhere

There is not a subject she shied away from. In "Like Animals," she writes about sex: "Over her like a dog / Muscular, tricky, neat." In "All the Princes of Heaven," she conflates the dawning of a new day with the various limbs and organs of a body waking to a tremendous erection: "Shooting stars and colored streamers / And twenty-one gun salutes / All the princes of heaven come / Leaping onto the land." In her last manuscript, she writes of a widow's aging body: "stiff thicket, scratched / sex the lie between the legs / prune dry and / curled / as if to open were possible / ever again." Her metaphors of the body are earthy, *defiantly* mixed, demonstrating in their wild leaps the body's own metamorphoses. She could mix her metaphors (her husband returned to her "a sense of balance / With water under my arms like wings") because she knew the body's betrayals. She could name it goat, horse, pig, dog. She could call it house, boat, glove. What was the self? What was the body that it could so often transform itself?

Most powerful are the series of cancer poems found in *Crossing the Same River*, beginning with "Illness as Metaphor," a poem dedicated to Susan Sontag, a writer who also died of cancer last year. "I know this is not really Ravensbruk," she writes. Yet, cancer *is* a holocaust:

And though I agree, in this century it is certainly irresponsible
Even to suggest that cancer is anything but superficially similar to a world
So sick it may not ever be able to cure itself.

In an early poem "In the Waiting Room," she speaks of "Carrying my illness to the hospital / Every day, carefully / As if it were a rare gift." The emotional honesty is breath-taking as she speaks of the narcissism that grave illness can evoke in us until we realize the other sick people around us: "I think I am something special but I am also numerous." She can be honest *and* funny. In the poem "In the Hospital," "robber / doctors . . . crawl out from under / lowering intestines / like mechanics wiping their foreheads / with soiled gloves." In poem after poem—"Princess," "The Same Slow Growth," "Hot Flash," and later in her poems about Leonard's decline in metal prowess, published in *When Earth Begins to End*, she confronts that which lesser poets would ignore or be embarrassed by:

> I would like to speak to you
> the way we used to,
> humming into each other's necks, close
> as tango dancers, step, glide
> embrace
> before you were dropped behind bars
> I can't get through.

What sustains courage and compassion in the face of such loss? The poems are not falsely transcendent, but transcendent, in any case. Love sustains her during the first bout of breast cancer in Mexico: "Though the life that pretends to float me / Is honeycombed with emptiness, great pits / The first hollowings of the disease . . ." she writes, "Because he says so it is easy / Simply to go right on bailing." Love reminds her that we are all in this grief-business together, that we are each left, at various points in our lives, to speak our unbearable grief "in this that was love's room." Whether it is the love she felt for her husband, Leonard, to whom all the books are dedicated after their marriage in 1968, or the love she felt for students, friends, the other people in the waiting room, it occurs and reoccurs in poem after poem, wedged right up against the cruelest facts of our human existence.

The dual nature of her seeing—the great themes of love and loss—also reveal themselves formally, in short lines that place fragments and stutterings, end-stopped and stressed, as in the way one thinks in grief—

> And this hill in the throat. To be walked over:
> all you ever wanted.
> Lie down, unseemly one. Would be too easy.
>
> "Northern Willow"

—and, alternately, in her long, loopy, indented, Whitmanesque lines and lists with their exclamations of praise, voices from the street, deer under the spruce, the path of neurons sparking, the multiplicity she celebrates. (As one critic wrote, she is a poet who believes in saying more, not less.) Hers is a poetry of "dis-equilibrium," in the sense the poet Robert Duncan speaks of it, as that which all living organisms strive to maintain. Evading equilibrium one evades death. Patricia's poetry, thus, is a poetry mapping the dis-equilibrium of being alive. Images, when not exactly careening, connect and divide and spark, much like the activity of the neurons she studied, the paths of perception which became the theme of her book *Invisible Horses*. It is a method which speaks to her life, as well. Her obituary, which appeared in newspapers across the country, claims, "She seemed sometimes to ski her own life, as if it were the most tantalizing and difficult slalom course imaginable; one that demanded (and rewarded) alertness and engagement at every turn." Peter Schjeldahl in a *New York Times Book Review*, states, "she has discipline and the nerves of a racing driver."

It can be exhausting to read. I imagine the trajectory of each book, as well as each poem, as the path of a bee or hummingbird, all zigzag, all contradiction, a-linear, impatient, a brilliant and yet *sown* order. The crazy, mixed metaphors she loved, like sharp turns down a slope, attach and detach at dizzying speed, as in "The Three Tortoise Secret of the World Power Plant" where the medulla oblongata that is at first found in the "cold, choppy" ocean inside us, becomes, in short order a "rainwater polished / shimmering sculpted block of marble," a sperm whale, "a solitary godhead, ticking," and soon is "chewing its underwater lips like a full moon caught in a trap." All in a stanza and a half!

Patricia loved conjunctions, the beautiful *and* of connection, connecting one thought to another, one image to another, one person to another. Many poems begin with the words *for, but, or, yet, and*, as if all experience was a conversation continuing, a meaning being made and continuously revised, even after the death of those with whom we were talking. Where does thought come from and where does it go? That thought was now discovered to be tangible, part of the body, fascinated her. She loved string theory, quantum physics. "I have spent most of my life trying to learn how to accept the fact that, as physics tells us, where there's a positive charge, contingent upon it there's 'always already' a negative charge," she writes in a statement for *Evensong*, a soon-to-be published anthology of poems on spirituality. "And vice versa. Trying to understand how to live in such a world, a world full of pain and suffering, I look to science, to string theory, to the implications of Mandelbrot's dazzling 'sets'."

The new physics gave her a language—even a theology—to speak of the self that suffers, that loves, that dies. It gave her a paradigm in which to ask the questions she was increasingly most concerned with: What is the self that is born from this swarm of origins and dies again into it? If with each moment everything is changing into something else, what can we hold onto? What is the individual self against such numerousness, such change?

> Because living
> or dead no one's home
> anyway, just left
> seconds ago, out the door to the beach,
> among the dunes glittering
> beyond all scatter as vast
> diamond pitted flakes scratch against each other.

> "Aftermath: Pinpoint and Torrent"

In her last published book, *As Earth Begins to End*, an elegiac meditation on grief and loss and a scathing protest against it, Patricia writes about losing Leonard first to the senility that claimed his lucidity and eventually to death. She writes of how it felt to wake to him gone, the depression still in the pillow. Where did he go? Where did they all go, the dead popping up like "black umbrellas" all over town? The scholar Robert Pogue Harrison, in his book *Dominion of the Dead* (a book Patricia was reading in the last months before her own death), writes that "The dead speak . . . as long as we lend them the means of locution; they take up their abode in books, dreams, houses, portraits, legends, monuments, and graves as long as we keep open the places of their indwelling." As this most amazing loss settles into the lives of the many people who knew and loved Patricia Goedicke, I like to think of her poems as places of indwelling, and that they will remind us not only of her but of "the beautiful names of all those / Who eventually will but must not / Entirely disappear."

—Melissa Kwasny
In Memoriam, 2006

ONE

Death be my home light. Turn night on its black
grindstone.

From sleep's sleepless engine
deliver me: who toys feebly with jaws,

who tricycles fast into false
        relief in a trompe l'oeil window.

In this that was love's room

who cries spectre come,
deck me, cuff me with spent fuses

soon enough dwindles from false dawn
        into false death wish or is it.

Sees who cannot. Fumbles for cracked glasses,

from cheating hat-trick
fitful dreams shot out

with no scythe yet
come whistling from the opposite corner,

that these chipped
under the lying stars dragged out
        hours of un-life be gone

come nearer, begs, come nearer.

THE BODY

Plump in its skin, sleek
as a boxing glove laid out

on a flat table, nose regal as the prow
      of His Majesty's clipper ship

becalmed. On a glassy bed of hardening
      veins, of blood marbled at the elbows,
         the vessel sits in its port.

            When did it stop?

In mid-motion. As in the children's game
called Statue,
        over a hidden hurdle flung, all bare teeth

and grimace, stiff legged
        as Picasso's fallen horses—

           When did it begin?

In mid-ocean.
And halfway round the world it snuck up on him.

Cold came. Then snow.
Veiled rooks sobbing.

The dealer, the ghost quarterback, called it
too soon, some would say—

And he?

Lips sewn shut.
Appalling fields of white.
　　　　To have come this far, to be still—

No more voices. No more wind in the rigging.
In the end, in the chill galley
　　　　the captain laid down his hand.

Who won?

But the decks were loaded.

HOLE

For if this be corpse

or grave. If this be tooth or cavity
or dry lake bed. Or spewed

self pity or howl, no tongue left
to speak with. If there be the same

killing fields from the start:
the gallows in the playpen

glares up at us like a black
graffiti covered

stone the day after

the execution. Birds like heavy cigars, coffins
wheeling overhead.

If there be cracked eggshell
and no egg. Neither yolk nor white

If there be no kernel. No core
to the applehead. If there be love

when love is dead.

If the outer firmament be arched
skin only. If the noose embrace nothing

but cold ore and bowels,

where is the high famed convexity
of which this is the concave?

For this is not a private. Not a personal
crack in a sealed container.

Not a single

lost shoe: on the nation's highways the owner
is long gone.

But whether this be outer
or inner rot, murderous

aimed or innocent kick, here

is an end to it, a hollow
depression which has no bottom

and no top.

NORTHERN WILLOW

I

But the tree in fall is even more glorious.
Candles, chains of yellow.
Outpourings of lament.

And this hill in the throat. To be walked over:
all you ever wanted.
Lie down, unseemly one. Would be too easy.

As if grief. As if rage. Below your feet
rocks howl in the mud.
Let them. There are other places

to arrive at. And if you did —
Lie down, unseemly. Contain yourself in the cellar.
There are children here

And windows full of stacked
finger bones. Neither will anger feed you.
So lie down. Rest.

Rock yourself to sleep. Over the rocks.
Hair falls in the river and is swept away.
You must not stop.

II

And must.
Here, where the seams
harden.

Ghosts take up their books
where they left them and go on.
Black lines snake their slow way

down tree trunks into veined
cavernous earth:
all mouth, all stomach

and no bells. Clang of no gold:
ecstasy and oblivion
chained between worm and sky.

So comb your hair. In the ocean.
In glass despair. In revulsion
let it. Freeze

over. But listen:
are we alone?
Dry leaves

scrape against the feet.
Stars with earth in their ears.
Though you would not believe—

Muscular roots reach down
from the faltering planets,
up from the ground.

THE QUESTION ON THE FLOOR

Some mornings the body wakes to itself
                              as to an ocean, the soft wash of it
            on a shore it wants to love. Lie back, love, it says,
                                        and let me lift you,
                  the sheets touching you are waves,

            the cool shock of first sun over the mountain lighting
                        the ceiling, then the floor—Ah yes, the floor

the body says, those skeleton boards
                        that trip and stumble us backhanded

But is this proper, is it mete?
            Especially after the calm miraculous
                        peace of the sea, say, after lovemaking

which never lasts, Horatio, never—

Though waves of liquid salt lap at each other, circulating
                  this tidal lymph (which is everywhere) is a mess
                              of needy corpuscles unmoored,
                  free form, floating—

As the great capricious Body above us moves on,
                              the question,
            is a tongue burning
                        to contain its own dissolving
            into snapshots

of what we used to look like: what cells
                              eventually consumed us
and what we cooked for the picnic, what blessings, how many oysters,
        or pancakes or kisses (which are words),

and more kisses, and more words, and more—
                        even as the great dunes,
            their chewed driftwood, and
        the entire shoreline falls out from under us.

L'CHAIM

But if you'd been pinched by it for years,
if inside that brittle package, your one
and only parched skin and bones there were scabs
scaling the inside of your nostrils, under your scrotum
if inflamed wrinkles scratched you at every step,

and if, after so long staring at it, trying
to prepare your family and yourself to just jackknife
into outer space and drown smoothly, barely stirring the waters,

it still wouldn't behave;
if deeper inside and always,
bending over the belt cutting into your gut
only to tie your shoes you felt the grinding

imperial Worm nudge upwards
hard against you as excrement and then, all at once
even as you straightened up, trying to ignore the distant
approach of vomit, cells gathering their undercover teams
for the daily seizure of *No Air, No Air;*

if the spavined wings of your lungs battered against your ribs
like trapped hail, if you thought
you'd never get your breath, goggle-eyed
beneath stretched eyebrows even as you rested,

if finally you raked your chest
frantic, no dignity left,

like a chicken
nailed to the bedroom floor, why wouldn't you go ahead and push

everyone aside, grab for the oxygen mask, in its plastic
rush of instant release, why wouldn't you just
take the powder you'd been waiting for all these years
and disappear, light as a rocket
after lift-off when the cellophane nose cone's sudden
quiet stopped up the one hole left in your life suit,
why wouldn't you leave behind

the faint parenthesis of your
mysterious smile, your domed scalp
wreathed by white hair as you finally turned away,

why would you even bother to look back
with a last flicker of tenderness for earth
and your wife and all your friends gathered at table
hushed, with everyone waiting for you
one more time to raise your glass, why would you?

AFTERMATH: PINPOINT AND TORRENT

A black dot, far away. The prick
and needled hiss of it. And the trickling, here on the beach
        as sky narrows to pupil. Garish

at the end of every light-shift
                  what's left but empty?

Gulled from the shore. As grackles shoot from a tree
shredded skirts rise. Black ash

flaps from a burning funeral pier;
smell of incensed seaweed.

As grit flies from flesh,
perspective's point dwindles,
to a cry: rasp of seashells.
        Implacable. Grinding, O

buffaloed, hurled from a mesa.
Slaughtered spirits extinct to what we don't know,

in the plod of daily bread we beg for it:
resurrection, *consummation*
            of the cindered body passionately to be

aroused. Born again into its own
seething somehow
           returned, returned—but No,

obviously. Cold slap in the face. Because living
or dead no one's home
                        anyway, just left

seconds ago, out the door to the beach,
among the glittering

beyond all scatter as vast
diamond pitted flakes scratch against each other—

(loud silence
of ants sipping water,
                        brittle grasshoppers breathing)—

As in a tape recorder's low
whispered undertow a snare drum's ghost

taps in and out, the foaming
of a once
            deep baritone voice attenuates itself

beyond the beach,
its frayed edges
                flickering

the outer eye motionless, in each cell
the mind's dendrites fly by
                    faster than any instrument can measure—

As riddled pinpoints flash,
static reflects what was
                    in bright cascading sparks

tiny geysers jet across small
empty intersections; plus, minus, positive
                              and negative both, as each speck splashes

for a few milliseconds in a circle scratched by a star
on a blind eye, the tail end of a smile

gathers and fizzes
into the abyss of it, radiant
                              black pinhole, torrent and vortex twisting

yes, where we converge
in the aftermath, with everything slowly settling

          and then rising, no surcease—

yet in the black sea of it, its syllables (strings in the wind)
in the frantic spittle of matter
                              in constant motion streaming,

in the watery spaces between us, cool sibillants
spit air and speak up:

stumbling along Oceanside Boulevard, listen,
even in strobed tears, between jeweled lightning shafts, *don't cry,*

as oblivion's traffic hisses,
all of us
                              into its bright grit churning

like mangled shorebirds, in the crash, whiplash and
jerk of convertibles, shiny steel caskets
        with their heads lopped off, *don't stop, look up*

go for the bull's eye, sight
right through it, pin the transparent

                black and white negative to the bull's eye.

THIS MUSIC HAS HOLES IN IT

but all music has holes in it.

rock plops into a pool
ripples spread for awhile

between the wickers of a basket   closings
then openings

none with any voice but the rock

plops into the pool
pool guzzles it delicious low throated gurgle

what does the air feel above it

child skips a stone into the water
        it's gone

then there's the cackle of a crow   the long arrogant
wail of a freight train
     passing

this house has holes in it
for looking out and in

      bubbles

where the glass blower paused

this heart has a valve in it
a hole   a slow leak

between seed and seed's descent
into its instrument

bow scratched across gut strings
fist in the chest   thud
                    and reverberations

this music has holes in it

big enough for a spaceship
          for a bomb
                    for a god to drive through

FROM THE BOOK OF SMALL ANIMALS

Mole on his low mound,
on his brushed doorstep stands

>> upright. Follows no light
>> But dim. On his own

recognizance,   balances
on the smooth rooftop

>> of the world he knows:
>> beneath him the tortured
>>> galleries he grubbed

> for himself alone, Eurydice
>> being long gone—

>> But he *had* to know. To see.
>>> Hadn't he?

And then wept.
Years. When once

> was more than enough: bitterest
>> of doomed storm-floods raging—

Then went on anyway. Learned
other ways to dig. To sing,

> we are told, this—

Mild monk. Respectable
watcher in the night—

On his dirt altar
flat-footed but lightly,

      with ten delicate toes grips
      the curved piece of earth he rests on: lifts up

his powerful short forepaws
to the sky and holds them there,

      his narrow head angled
          slightly, never mind what

he can't see but feels, possibly—a distant
warmth?

           —or some faint
           probing pulse

      of finned current, invisible
      scent of wild honeysuckle

all around him, rarest
of rare chrisoms reaching for him, yes him:

      thumbless.   in a strange wind.

TWO

Six feet by three feet patch
swells upward, slightly
greener toward the chest.

Plastic carnations, polka dots.

Behind, tall wheat,
some pines, a ragged fence

and the occasional clink clunk
of the cow bells we hung here

once, when I came out
with my friend, her two blonde babies
tumbling, one still at the breast—

But you are nowhere in evidence, down there
dressed in the green sweater I knitted for you
when we first met.

On the horizon, 350 degrees of raw mountains;
the passing brush of wind—
sunshine's glint.

At the center, a handful of whiskery
wild roses in a pot

and a clump of sunflowers that burns
like a yellow warning light, stuck, swinging
in the middle of a deserted intersection

surrounded by old ranch houses, faint flecks of snow
still visible on the mountains.

There are many benches
    and many intersections, and your father lives there
   and your mother, and now you,

you benched there, in the silence
    where monoliths jab the skyline—

      Unstoppable seizures of grief

But who is it who has not
    rubbed shoulders with someone oddly familiar
   and hardly noticed it; isn't it possible everyone meets everyone

at least once again
    without knowing it, for one second in a whiff,
      a barely perceptible feeling of ships
     passing each other on the radar?

The Queen of Spades coughs. Cuffs me
    with the back of her hand into black ink:

  it is the blood of your death I write with and cannot get out of.

Here in my study, with its rickety
    white speedflower of a fan stirring things up
into jerky film strips, sneaked visions of you whirring
  in the tiny breeze it steaks across my face
    I can't help it, it goes on

even in your absence, ink
   still flows, the air hose is oxygenated and keeps moving,

in the broken diving bell of your death it is your element
   I breathe through until we are both in it, released
finally from ourselves . . .

Because curled in my ear, your voice
   is the glistered path of a snail, is rainwater,
  is wet tires hissing in the street, is wisps of air

is seeds stuck to the teeth, the first letter of a word
   on the tip of everyone's tongue

though no one says it; in the garden, in the glint
   of reflected light, of spores drifting dry-eyed

from the tallest flower of the onion family,
   the fuzzy lavender head, the lovely bloom

like a monstrance on its altar: fluttering, shy, floating
   on its single stalk nodding to us

 nodding to us?

Doubtless I wish too much, and flowers are no more priests
  than the Queen of Spades

Well, I am battered.
   But the rational world is a lie, and the twin cities
of Heaven and Hell too—.
   and this is my dream in the middle.

On the bed everyone lies on, still
                        in the end or the beginning,

with the last neurochemicals of feeling, anchorless ideas
                in the scent between us lingering

in the high bedroom, under the ceiling fan, with far off
                        muffled cars honking, great bunches of rustling
                green leaves still sway, still sweep across the roof,

in such in and out patterns
                        as fountains make,
                delicate fugues muttering,

in such intersections of light and then shade,
                        in these flying specks, in the mind's streaming

vast inner city traffic, it is the blood
                        not of your death but of who we are together
and not together I write with and cannot get out of.

Sooner speak to the moon than to what
                        is not a body: under its light lunatic
            in our aspirations, solar
        in our sorrows, O Oriole, O Warble,
                        waver and warp of time's stringed
                                nuclear musiks, forgive me
                    my staring emptiness if I stand mute, listening
                    for what I cannot hear.

Under the heavy drone of the midnight
            passenger plane from Salt Lake City, its thin tinkling voices
        high above me, in shadowy maples rustling,
                    on a dark corner of the world even a girl's laugh breaking
            like sea spray across a quiet street
        is barely intelligible to anyone O radiant
                    all-around-us Rainbow of sight and sound,
            if these rippling harmonics, these rosy corals
                        and fluted silks, if these pertain to You,

O Stars, O Atoms, tremble, O You
                of the so many you's in You, how dare
                    a single I even on your arm dream
        of entering such an impossible *pas de deux,*
                    even in your unbounded
                leaping spaciousness exchange
                one step, one passing
            intricate figure out of millions, one
                terrified word with You?

Yet I must approach; I know
                no nothingness more stringent, no matter more
          teeming with paradox than yours: down to your most
                    miniscule/majestic,
      in the foaming vortex of You
         see how one of your least
leafy green bonfires crumbles me into wordless
                hollow digits:

in linked zeros though I babble, please
         may my orisons be manifold
      enough; else how may I speak
              in what multitudes of static
        in whose eely electric tentacles do we sparkle O

I am not big enough
     I have fear
            in my smallness ever to say
     even my great gratitude   my terror
       even my willingness to wait   how long
    to be admitted to You   or never   why
   should You bother to   speak to us
       desperate ones who cannot listen is it possible it is
also You
     who cannot engage, O most profligate

efflorescence of
     seed   space-worm   crabbed nebula
      and starry perseids down beaming
        all its proteins braided

into your glass
colliding passages of speaking
out of so many mouths, to whom
should I speak,
in which of your many languages, which digit in the many i-ed
trillions; one, zero
forgettable tens of thousands of us, streaming
lost lovers, parents and babies in bits,

O Sidereal, O Galactic, O Skeletal X-Ray Hand,
You who could wear us all
on one finger like a dime store ring winking
from knuckle to studded brass
battlefields of bloodied infants to glittering
chill dazzlements of light, from clenched polar peaks
to drowned volcanoes, in these your imperial
slippery ways, O You

to whom I cannot pray   personally   please
help us to find uncover You at last,
for a moment may we be comforted equally
at each end of the binoculars
trembling, small and large
fused to You though we are lost, beyond all reason
at these extremities of vision, which is it
or anyone   keeps us apart
at least let me imagine we could meet even speak
on some crackling frequency, if not these
whatever it is brings us
to these shimmering transparencies, this veiled, light-struck
Aurora,
the radiant evanescence of your knees

crack of dawn in the bathroom
as usual at the sink
blear eyed ache of waking
the face saying Yes, Okay
come along old soul,
co-pilot, distant   friend from my mother's womb
pick up your pen   whisper what was meant
from the beginning   present
and then not   and then again, this
slight rustle in the brain-rigging   hint
of an off-shore breeze in the chest-sails

next minute at breakfast
gone slack   forgot
in an hour or two back
in sync again   for another
star turn   glowing   who said
filaments can't burn   even when the light's
off   who said connection

means to be lost   well
it is   dammit what's happened
to it now   here's only
the silk lining of the ring box
where the swift, unsalted   one
all day comes and goes humming
fitfully   it's a relationship
not a thing

thumbnail creature that won't
stand still
except at the window   pale lip
of the mind flower   next second
off again but be patient   put honey out
at noon   try sighing   intermittently

don't worry about attending
to everything   just remember
every little while   tap at the door
of the busy, crammed with duties
can't stop head, the chock full
redbreast pounding for air   a little room to sit
still in   sometimes something will say
hello   take my hand   this is
what is meant   and then not   and then again
follow

A year and a half after you died I looked up from my novel—
                        another one about Pygmalion and Galatea—
      and once again you were nowhere.

There was a kind of soft crash in my stomach,
a sense of no air,
               (or rather, nothing *but* air—)

then I was inside a giant soap bubble and I kept pressing,
                  to see or hear or touch at least something
                     but there was nothing.

So I decided to take a walk barefoot through the summer evening,
to see how far this feeling of emptiness,
                  of the world holding its breath, would stretch—

But the walls kept moving away, transparent lungs
         ballooning softly through the neighborhood where we used to walk.

With stereos once in awhile thumping, from a few cars driving by,
         or children calling, stones bumping against each other, far off,

I tried to see into them, the lives behind the fences
and the little neat houses on the block but it was you I wanted,

not these people passing, nor the blank windows I went by
         slowly, dragging each naked foot through the air—

It was as if I were under water, drowning
                    but still alive, looking up through the crystal surface

high above to the twilight over the treetops
where I watched my life with you passing and I wanted it back—

—And yet there was still, there is always
something, I insist at the very least

a sense of shelter from the maples
                    slanted over the sidewalk, the apricot sky—

In this tawny silence, with the flushed face,
the wit, the brisk crackle I loved
                    all gone back where they came from, scattered into air,

sprinklers still hush the grass, the walls move in and out,
                    in the neighborhood where we used to walk

there are no voices but yours and I can't hear you
                    as I weep for you and move towards you and through you.

AT THE EDGES OF EVERYTHING, CRACKLING

in almost tidal movements,
               people crowding together
     back and forth   shifting

looks given   then taken away
          hooks and   uneasy whispers
              trickling out from the faint fringes of things

fiery sun matter   invisible
         sways from one planet
    one shoulder   to another

passing each other   cats
         slide through doorways
           in opposite directions tingling   fine hairs   rise

cells heave outwards
         towards other cells
           at the edges of everything   crackling

exiles hide in the passes
         brandishing their   cell phones
          armies call across canyons

meteors in space flash
         across the   helmless
          radioactive fields

oscillant specks
                in each closed system connected
                                  somewhere   o far star

So, my
dear, intransigent One. Still
    in the dark.

All we lived for rides,
    rides

below,
    deep as a snout, sub–
        marine silent.

But if there is no
answering sign from the body
    beside us as we sleep,

never sure
    if it is there
        or not; well is it?

—Beyond time. And within it:
    ebony cold
    needle. Next to a damp match.

All day anchored to it
    without knowing:

so fast the fire
    throttles itself into ash.

Above, the little yacht
flaps its gaudy pennants, plies its bright orange
            over-the-counter trinkets:

how else live, speak
            as one must, to others?

Yet in the midst of company near
            collapse the

tweak of tears threatens
                    to spill, spoil the illusion

that it's not here, whatever
                        surges up from the bowels

daily and is repressed
            or not repressed;

the sealed mouth that yawns
                    wide open, the stomach

that grinds continually, begs only to be fed
forever:
                this hunger

of all things most monstrous
            and most dear

howls at the wind and then wades
right into it,

the emptiness of a ghost ship, an entire lit city
sunk, with all its thousand
                    and one lights blinking

like eyelids. Body within body
                    waterlogged, barely moves,
                drifting in the neural currents

where nothing's whole but
split. Palms up, slightly
                    swaying. With so many frayed synapses

still firing, in memory's clanging hull
                        strewn with so many meteors, spent coins
                scattered across the floor

where all rowboats foundered,
                all vessels bump,
                nudge against each other, softly

in the one bed where the treasure
                once opened, never closes but rides, rides
            below us, in the dark.

THREE

But real. As goatskin. As leathery
                    pomegranate packed with seeds circulating through
          all of us, you were sweet sap, apple; even in old age
                    never drained, fine high jet of conversation

endlessly rising and falling, no I am not
                    exaggerating here: you were articulation's
          juiciest man loaded
                    with salts crystallizing into sugars, into hard

fragrant cider: even sagging from the heart-stem
                    painfully, at the apparent end you were still full of it,
              spirits that never sting but speak true, brisk buckups
          for darkening friends, fruit flies and honey bees multiplying
              around you

then as they do now, under leafless trees stricken,
                    jostling each other for one more sip of you.

LETTER TO . . .

I can't think
except by halves   now

like everyone   cut off
who shouldn't have been   why stop   trying

pencil stubs   used matches
maps of hair flattened

once there was a you here
in the back yard

under the giant spruce like a clipper ship
surging against stars

I try to see
blindfolded to the fire

lit candles   loose cascades
streaking across the firmament

the tall chariots above us
in the trees a dark swinging

of crystal constellations
invisible calligraphies circling

only what isn't
to be seen

snowflakes melting
skeletons in a mirror

looking for each other's
etched reins   twins

so many jeweled meteorites
in wet branches   in the morning

flashing their brief   brilliant digits
to you   me   no one

who can decode them

NIGHT NOTES

(Fall 2002)

stiff thicket, scratched
        sex the lie between the legs
   prune dry and
         curled
      as if to open were possible
   ever again under a dog moon
         ponderosas rasping
           on the road between mirrors
   that say nothing   no voice
    in the dust depths of camphor and cottonwood
     tunnels
  this envelope full of scraps
        waiting to be answered

      throw them into the wind like ash
      gray sails after an unconsummated ceremony

on the back porch where the cats
   loll on an elderly labrador
        no stars
   raw flags of wind tell me to stop
    doing what I'm not doing and look
     at a few snapshots

·ᴗ

at scrabble, spitting words
                like sparklers, Russian-Jewish firecrackers
         for me and your feisty
    older sister   sometimes she'd win a game
    but not often   you were a master
               now she's gone too

      perhaps she'll be there later
  when I join you

·ᴗ

probably no one joins anyone
              here or   after
     but whatever last
   formlessness you've become
  still I go spidering
      straight out after you on my own
 white hair whispering
            along its strands inching
      ghost sister   ghost
           wife
  trying to find you and turning
            slowly into a dead tree
     form of buried seed

VEGETABLE 69

such a ragged old onion you wouldn't
recognize me   all these years
I hope

wispy hair stuck up
like twigs out of a nest

dry skin flaps   bags
of undigestible matter
in a bin with all the other Picasso

bug-eyed shoots sidling
out of left too long vegetables

near death I suppose everyone is
naked

without makeup   losing it
even my clown red
lipstick

line drawn against encroaching
wrinkles from nose to chin

seriously I can't   quite
see
sallow gray dishrag me

potato-eyed in the dark
soft-hearted   smart

just feeling around

KAYAK

Shoe without a foot.
Moccasin shaped, sealskin
      soul pod. Knocking against the dock.

Leaf, scatter of lackadaisical cloud—

but you were never a hard driver.
          Nor I either.

Filled, used to be
both of us,
      whole from stem to stern.

Some days, sailing along,
I'd carry you with me, from subway to work and back
      like a book I couldn't put down.

Other days, folded close
we'd turn ourselves upside down in the river
      and just hang there, sputtering,

then swing right back up again—amazing—
and never drown.

Drifting along as one
welded, spirit-caulked,

so fitted feels
wet. Sleek

easy as fish feel,
tail and fin powerfully
                swimming upstream—

or womb-walls, caressed. Rippling
so smoothly who knew which was which—

Except for the villagers on the banks,
the children calling out

across the world:
little pot-bellied chocolates
            trampled in their sandboxes—

Who paddles for them?

While you and I ate, drank,
lifted and dipped arms

who said any great enterprise, even love, say
                is worth *how* many
lives?

Reader without a book to read by.
Glass without water. Plate without a crumb—

Last night you came swimming towards me across the desert.
Rudderless. But still sea-going.

Bother the big ships, the ocean liners full of people.

Who said one isn't
as good a crew as two.

Frail memory vessel for
ghost texts, palimpsest almost forgotten

children,
tender Pharaohs
"forever"—

word stitched across
on thin papery skin.

Open, please, and let
a live body in.

Come, Shoe. Tongue, wag your best.
This isn't a coffin
                    yet.

With or without paddles,
each life's leavings
              call, imprinted deep

in stem and marrow dreaming
single cell on the sea
                still knocking, full of—

covered and sealed
for the night.

FOUR

Soft caramel to the tongue, this
chewy trifle life—

and no remedy for it,
such sweets unfit

     for soul to suck on:

At first we lapped them up,
the lazy strawberry beginnings,

later even the fake No Salt
offered to failing hearts, but *then!*

       Spat them out, had to: couldn't

stomach it, sweet friend, since you left us, no

tender nothings, no
lollipop, no

easeful placebo can syrup over
such an Absence as this—

     rot. This sour

drop. Pothole. Bitter chocolate
chip the sick Dealer deals all of us.

EACH MOMENT

but even as languid islands   medallions of luminous   jello
on the surface of the sea   sway

with no more birth streamers
to tie us   down

gently we are
       also

small planetary blobs
     of palm oil or olive

on the face of time   passing
in and around   ourselves

in slow swells   what consciousness we have
product of a smooth digestive system   Whose

peristalsis   mine   ours
yours   is what matters

the days we spent   spent
dissolved into the liquid

eye of the mind   lazy
after-images   only?

"These fantasies can be interpreted
easily"   F explains

lubricious but not lucent
enough   not haloed

in his eyes not even felt
              through

garages of shimmer
                    dangerously greased rags

the plates of our lives drift
              in sinister green

thin carpets wallowing
              sodden but not quite   sunk

in contaminated oceans rising
                    to swallow us

in the city's lurid   rainbows
                    what we see we look through

our bleared selves   each moment always
              opalescent   a seagull   balancing

on a spreading oilslick
                    settling its feathers   unruffled

softly   we who are pressed
          jasmine   violet in the evening

in morning's yellow citron
                              glowing

in late afternoon dried
          cactus needles us   back

into cold   heaving salt   but calm
                    the husks of what we were

rootless   through steep waves
          roaring over us   riding them

with bobbing heads   occasionally
          shipwrecked but not often

mostly distilled   essential
          blooms of coconut   gardenia   peanut

sweat and musk swaying
                    back and forth on the subway

in bed 2 backed   with lovers
          finding   then losing

in retrospect what does it matter   we are all brilliant
                    blurred ovals of light passing

so fast they are   slow
          against the night a single

glittering belt of light
               flashes before us   immense

invisible platters of dazzle
          swimming around the world

headlights streaming
               at twilight down Park Avenue

archipelagoes   of consciousness
          unconscious
               compact of all colors

MOON SONG

last night the moon was sneaking around
playing tricks

all over the house   first at the East windows
then at the West
               probing the rooms here there

what would she be
without the god shining on her
               with his heavenly   flashlight

was it you I recognized   or the death
riding on your shoulders
               drew me to you

which is which   for any of us
on day's heels death
               the always coming on   the black rock

illuminated
only by love following   hard after

breathing on it   caressing it
to a high gloss   globed against silver cliffs

                     ⌣

day in   day out which   is it
the dark escalators up   to the Brilliant City

     or the tunnels beneath it   subways
odorous rat highways those tearing apart forces
that bear us only to push us up

headfirst   from wormroot
to million eyed weeds   to murder us

sooner or later   tanks prowling the streets
giant gun barrels at the door

where everyone gathers   at last
breaking the silence

will it be the doorbell with its faint
t-r-ill of welcome   the tiny chime

at the altar for the raised Host
or   just after

         .◡

this morning the moon's peering in at me
at 7:00   pale glittering plate
      over the sycamores waitin only to go out

these days I hear little   deaf
even to the telephone ringing

friends tell me I've shrunk
to a quarter of myself   remembering

on the pillow was it your face   elegant

Greek profile of a vase
or the space around you   empty
air holding you   in place

when the beloved vacates the premises
all one dares

ask for is death
light   on his shoulders

I've no idea what's coming   or how or
when

only that if it has two sides at least
one of them must be you

CLOUD CHAMBER AND CIRCUMFERENCE

Each morning now the sky opens
                              silent, neutral,
          without you

yawns. Stretches its mouth wide
as a gray cat.

                         ·᷄

A band of defeated cavalry,
          a few grandmothers straggle past

and the silence begins again. On the Steppes of Russia
                    the fighter jets scream by,

laser beams sweep the horizon
                    like Geiger Counters, black holes

that never stop dissolving, eating themselves up, inky caps
          drowning in their own blood—

                         ·᷄

Even when we knew, or thought we knew you were here,
often you were so busy, absorbed in the machinery of light

and how it got here, each glint prickling
from one jumping off point to another,
                              of course it seemed you were elsewhere.

From second to second in your thoughts,
who knew where you'd gone, under which constellation

which sweater would you wear, everything is so
                              complicated, so un-present

everywhere, ions invisibly flicker
inside every skull bone, even the stillest,
                          from one cerebral colony

to the next, where's anybody right now, especially you:
          you told us the gods wouldn't be telling

                              ·‿

and they aren't;
the sky turns coal colored, turns shot
          velvet with orange shear,

and the censors come down like shades,
the photographer's heavy cloth
                          reverses, inks out all light

but what we are told to see, barely a scrap
to guess at, something blurry
                  beyond the kitchen window, on a far perimeter

no one catches or even notices, for all our butterflied nets,
our cramped, secret

stalactite corpses in the closet growing up
or is it down,

who really remembers that the sky goes on beyond us
forever: at the end of a northern street

mountains hunch themselves at the heavens,
the Steppes stretch away into nothing, dogs curl up and sleep
       under the sun's veiled eye as ready to flick awake

·╯

as you were, at the slightest movement
from the picture window noticing each leaf, taking in
       each student on the sidewalk jostling by,

in the wide cloud chamber of your mind scanning for every least
     skeletal spirit-shape of feeling

electric in the air around you as lightning,
as dazzled corposant patches, short circuiting

but still flashing, in the tall rigging reared up
high over the bridge of thought where you strode
      in all weathers relaxed, easily balanced

captain of your own whale-tossed ship, your blue, infinite
sea-changing eyes wide open,
      ranging the rim of the world.

KALO TAXIDI, FUERA Y MAINTENANT

If we could only fit into
            each other. If just
        one of us could—smooth as grease slide
     into another and stay there,

Vitreous green
          pitcher. Foot.
      And cup: the exact cradle
              shadow evaporates out of, wavering
     stretched sail going nowhere.

But now you have jumped ship, soundless, glimmering,
             the remaining passengers lie in the hot nights
      grappling in each other's arms

or pin only, wrinkled
          frail tissue paper patterns over the faint troughs,
     the hollows of the bed you lay in—

                the buttocks, where they were;
                the shoulders, how they feel
                without you—

And the absent head, in the squashed pillow's
          dented cupola, its once intricate
     hum even as you slept, *where has it all—*

Untouchable.
Atomic jukebox of bee stings, *when is nothingness
not,* and where—

into every galactic belt of cold light
withheld, O *withheld*—

*That the glass bowl of space.
That the infinite's envelope seal in itself
at least one of our scribbles—*

let us inhabit each other however
untranslatably we can:

Je (can be) *l'espace ou tu etais,
et je* (will become) *nous:*

cargo and hold, swift cutter,
flying vanquisher over grief's
heaving wallows, its leaky scatter and ooze –

*Mientras, amor mio,
las lagrimas se vuelven gaviotas,*

over strewn garbage,
over picnickers on the beach wheeling, O
Well turned, Tern!
—a joke only you could have shouted, grinning

for the sport of it, pleased
as if you'd done it yourself, at the doubling

swift shadow above you, the wings
    scissoring over you where you had leapt up
     and were, and were not

  the bird itself; in hand

or already loosening, from thumb and clutched fingers
      the spirit slipping away among high
   teetering white sheets over the horizon, you

in whose bed we would lie forever,
    who once stood tall in yourself as a building,
    in your own
      blocks-long footprint—

    if I were you *(si yo fuera tu)*
    if I were really you *(si vraiment j'etais toi)*

then soon we'd be back together, tucked into the same
   checkered lightning of the cab you took yourself off on

    (safe journey) *querido—*

and left us weeping, by the oil-soaked harbor calling
    like sad tankers groaning, in broken animal Morse

    Ecoute! Oiga!

but still the gulls cluster,
    rasping on gritty decks
   or perched on teetering antennae, in every *courant d'air*

winged neurons, garbled angelic axons
still making identity's raucous, near unintelligibly
coded secret connections—

Mais qui es ce qui s'appelle je, moi
ou toi?

In every feathered hollow,
in yours, where you once rested and were
and are still; in wing, petal, fishtail,
in every waxed and honeyed
echo chamber hidden, each articulates in its own
blood and chlorophyll and bones the dear,
uncrackable,
many-in-one-tongue you have vanished
and not vanished from.

TRACE

We live on the cusp of knowing:

        is what happened
      or the merest hint of it not
anything?

Edged on either side equally   before / after
      how *do* they disappear,
           deliquesce, then divide
   into cells that multiply,   doubled
          smoke rings pale circles
      rising into the sky?

Most want back
    secretly, only one
        and in particular; one familiar breath lit
  briefly, on a warm cheek,   one hand
    full of live corpuscles,   *not lost*
      in the blur and wash of time—

        So eons pass.

Stars sprinkle themselves
      like dandelions over the lawns but in 2 weeks
  fluff up into dust,
    into vague seed pods that wander off

Nor is it possible to find anyone out there
                or even in here, but hidden
        in minds
                like fish in weedy tanks, in haircuts less and less
                brilliantined, in scuffed sandals abandoned

on summer porches to moths,   random wings,
                The stuttering synapses of age fibrillate
                        in someone's skull always,
            even in a sandstorm the first two syllables
                    of a known footstep might crackle
            like static on a broadband   quick flashes, inklings
                    at the tip of nothingness, still:

FIVE

For who struck first and where, in what joint
       of clock time never matters.
          When so many of them come
   everywhere thudding in, what's worst
            is nothing's to be done about it

but swallow hard. Forget. Suffer
       doer and done to both
    sunk into a hissing pot, the hot metal
          quickly smothered, oh quickly—

But the eerie way they vanish! Shot star
       across the night blackened,
    by day hardly noticed:
          innocent minor excrescence, swollen
      gland, tree burl
        trapped in an irritated throat—

So self seals itself up
       as it must, to keep itself whole.
    Ignorant, in forced
         necessary sleep, the healthy system digests
     its own illness first, then others':
   scabbed corpses covered,
        pothole arteries clogged

with denial: *all things blow over*
       eventually, the houses sit back up,
   the cars go back to work as usual—

But the dropped stitch still simmers
        heedless, underground
    in forests of acid rain, the slow seep
        of wrinkles across fair cheeks,

the stock market clangs shut,
        at first closing and then again, for which market
    when, around the timed world ticks
        blow by blow, as the wind settles and shifts

in Delphic caves. In Stygian
        wine cellars. In London. Hiroshima. Manhattan,
    all poisonous growths encapsulated
        only to be spat out

year after year, as each stifled madness,
    each new wave finds itself
        coming even as it's going, and vice versa,
    at the stroke of Radioactive High Noon

Surprise! Horror grabs us;
        stunned, in vicious gusts pummeled
    from Cape to Cape, from ear to burning ear tacking

back and forth, from one barricaded
        safe harbor, one mass coverup
    to the next, never to rest
        ever: how far a single shadow can reach
    is not to be known by day, *O mio babbino caro,*
as the world blows itself away.

My flicker, my once chipper of crisp woody flakes
in time's mills dulling down—No, Not You—
       Nicht, Verboten,
   among the doves in the gutters slurred

outside everyone's window nodding, bobbing
           among all our lost nobodies—

And yet the air's full of you.
       Names names names
   flash across the screen, slow portraits in their paid-for silences

on Channel 12 or Al Jazeera, men blindfolded, and women
        rubbled. A scarecrow hangs by its plucked throat—
       So the lost are found.

But if entropy has its way, or love—
   Steel needles wobble, revolve in the wind like gallows.
   Against the wall, *al paredon!* Generals

and civilians blazing, then incinerated,
      even my own now
   non-combatant word-soldier
      with his one trickster leg and no dog-tag—

as specks of split energy, of bitter,
   of brutally sweet sweep in radiant waves over the mind's sieves

Stop. Stop again, and listen
to the world's secret magnets, hidden valences nodding
                        from pole to pole to Hungary, bad joke
            and no joke:

as Sanskrit turns in the deep
            Himalayas out to the North star which is where
                exactly, at any given moment depends on where we are—

and you too, my brave phantom bird,
                    my guardian ghost beak among us always, turning
            (if entropy has its way, or love)—

by fits and starts in each lookout, each satellite's tall vaults,
                    in the cold sky we are caught up
        all of us, from how many barracks, how many innocent houses
numbered

myriad as fleas. As spirit-specks hopping,
                pressing against the atmosphere like rain
                    withheld, always withheld—

Yet in the veiled galaxies drifting, still minimally breathing—why not—
                in long transparent rows like the young Koestler's
impossible
            canopy of the dead circling above us, toe to head to toe

all around us, in thin force-fields invisible, unencompassed
            great migratory flocks of birds sweeping by—
                        out there where there is nothing. *Nothing.*
            And no emptiness.

Overnight the too late ambulances,
a few more black umbrellas pop up and disintegrate
        in small gases, short puffs

now like a rash, now like a cluster bomb of blisters
                        over the railroad tracks—

See how the fragments come down
delicately?
                Horrifying as ash. First a femur,
                then a smile, then an eyelash—

Or crickets, hopscotching
in and out of the mild
        milky squares we jump around in after them,

large suns squeezed into smaller bodies, barely discernible
                selves like scarred moonscapes seen from within
        and darkening, into thinner and thinner slices

or never. Or right here. Think
kaleidoscopes revolving,
                opposing parallels that never pause,

not even for the kindest of saints' countenances dipping
and bowing, pinned to the tall banners

in their royal papier mache processions hiding from us,
                dodging behind rooftops and cornices vanishing—

When it knocks it knocks rapidly. Sharp
one after another stilettos. Machine guns in the distance
   but coming closer, exploding around us like pillows,
  entire cities of feeling peppered across white sheets—

Yet in a year or two smudged.
Out on the lawn grubbing, amiable moles
   nudge up under us

like footsteps in the backyard
  strange stepping stones meandering

among white mushrooms sprouting,
faint spores trailing out of sight
   to the far ends of the galaxies and down Main Street

on All Soul's Night even among witches, even the Mayor as Merlin
   with wings flapping, leather overcoats,
  sinewy swallow tails silhouetted

as benigh blips, UFO's whizz by
   off the memory screen into stale candy
  in numb brain pockets rubbing dully against us—

     ·‿

And then easier.
Though the smell is still of slick, broken
   thick fingerbones, the whiplash of loose lightning
jabbing at the horizon,

they keep coming, but softer.
In the taste of twilight cigarettes drifting
        across the grass like Myrmidons, hobos at the back door,

whether we notice them or not, they keep tapping:
behind the eyes whispering, each night and not just in the movies
            a series of serious men and grave women in top hats
        on skinny unicycles wobbles across the sky and disappears

over and over, for the world's windows are transparent,
the couple across the way forever yaps
    over their tea-time martinis, with the cat snoring in the corner
  later they make love, shedding inhibitions and clothing

everywhere, small flecks of bare skin,
            even after they move on they remain

in pieces all over the house. In bureau drawers,
in desks. On the back stairs, especially in the glassy
                whirlpool depths of mirrors
        continually changing places, out there
                        on the dark grid of the lawn.

THE BASEBALL FIELD AT NIGHT

but what keeps us company   is not
always here   the bare space
where the cat was is simply

where   if there was a voice
in a corner of the world it's gone
said something   then hung up

so call back   ask
nobody wants to cross an absolutely empty
baseball field at midnight   probably not even   you

if you were here gangs of   crows hover
in the shadows   never mind the abandoned
car by the roadside

spiked with wishes   stars
motorcycles to repair   and orphanages
full of skinless   small you's crying

what keeps us fatherless
and motherless   each in our air-tight
body capsules   zipped   the cities of time are full

of friendly taxi drivers   where do they go
when they're not talking   or listening
over the radio grid to the score keeping

the churches won't do
these days or to the stock market's
stranglehold on the soul's economy

if there's no company coming
for supper to share the   jug wine
can a single self   bless itself

but maybe it doesn't   have to
when two breaths meet   sighing out
sucking in

over the plate   sometimes   at the tip
of the disappearing bat
suddenly there are three

and more than three   the night's diagrams
are more faceted than black
diamonds revolving   a single player strikes

more than out   the doorbell
sometimes rings and there's no one   only an extremely
peculiar hair-on-the-back-of-the-neck

feeling of something or someone
wanting what, change   a few bucks
to save the world   spin it

on its three bases glittering   towards home   wherever
that is   such complicated
strings stretch between us   doubled   then tripled

in a cat's eye cradled
from point to point flashing   what if the cab driver really
does know where we're going

the vacuums of space hum   with so many different
baseball fields   mysterious   dark
matter   vast plateaus of cold

and hot   bristling spheres flying
back and forth   here
and not here   only wait

sometimes over the hard packed
emptiness between triangles
there's an ocean and we're in it   occasionally

a warm   dragging   mountainous swell comes
out of nowhere   if there is actually
such a place

or an end the wave doesn't know
beneath our dangling feet elegantly   lifts us
a little nearer toward   where

ENVOI

little sweats sneak up on her   creased
                    on the mushroom green duvet
            where his desk used to be

the old furnace gasps itself to life   trembles
                              every fifteen minutes or so
                sudden exfoliations   puffs
                              coverlet full of feathers

no, don't   he wheezed
            laughing
into her firewall trunk   her button-hole eyed
                sewing box her big   empty brain

glue, stick   but *Hold*
            that we may be held

as worlds tear themselves   apart
                the cracked chandelier reflects
            every atom   multiplied
                paper   books   skin crashing   through

                Ad astra
                And higher

only put your hand on my   she cries out
                              remember the thorned oath
                we did not   swear

stars   palaces of flame
                                    crossing into open blackness deep
            turbulences   in the zone between what and
                        what

without you all lights go out
                        and on and on

            without any of us all lights go out
                                    and on and on

"From the Book of Small Animals"
for Constance J. Poten, after Philip McCracken's *Mole Greeting the Sun* (bronze)

"The Blow"
"O Mio Babbino Caro" from Puccini's opera, *Gianni Schicchi*

"Yet Compass Me"
"the young Koestler's impossible canopy"—from Koestler's *Darkness at Noon*

"Heliopause In His Study Now Her Bedroom"
heliopause is a term used by scientists to describe the turbulent zone that occurs
between the outer edges of the solar system and the realms of interstellar space

"a single cricket"
from an anonymous haiku translated by Yasuko Horioka

a single cricket
chirps, chirps, chirps
and is still